EASY AMAZON FBA GUIDE

HOW I EARN AN EXTRA $2,000 PER MONTH SELLING BOOKS PART TIME ON AMAZON!

BY ETHAN FROST

Copyright © 2016 by Ethan Frost. All Right Reserved.

No part of this publication may be reproduced, distributed, or transmitted in any form or by any means, including photocopying, recording, or other electronic or mechanical methods, or by any information storage and retrieval system without the prior written permission of the publisher, except in the case of very brief quotations embodied in critical reviews and certain other noncommercial uses permitted by copyright law.

TABLE OF CONTENTS

Chapter 1. Why Sell Books on Amazon FBA?

Chapter 2. Scanning

Chapter 3. Book Sourcing (Where to find books to sell)

Chapter 4. Best Types of Books to Sell for Profit

Chapter 5. Sales Rank and Pricing on Amazon

Chapter 6. Book Grading and Condition

Chapter 7. Packing and Shipping your Books to Amazon

Chapter 8. Conclusion

Introduction

I have been selling books on Amazon FBA for about 3 years. I have learned a lot since the first days of my Amazon FBA book selling journey and it is amazing how much I've learned over the last couple years. The good news is that I have given in this book, a good outline and basic steps to duplicate or even surpass what I have done selling books on Amazon FBA. In order to succeed book selling you will have to actually start the process yourself and get going. You will not be an expert right away or understand perfectly everything I explain in this book.

The top things you need to know is that :
1. You must source and find good books
2. You need to set your price and send the books in to Amazon
3. You need to track how your books are doing and check how the books you are selling are doing (are they selling well?)
4. KEEP REPEATING STEPS 1 TO 3

Of course there are myriads of other details that you must know about and I have discussed many of them in this book. But the main thing is to get started and start selling books on Amazon as soon as you can.

Chapter 1. Why Sell Books on Amazon FBA?

Are you unfamiliar with Amazon FBA? It is a program where you set up an FBA account with Amazon. You then list products (books in this case) and ship them into one of Amazon's warehouses. You then wait for your items to sell on Amazon.com and when they do, Amazon picks, packs, and ships them to the customer who ordered it. Amazon will also handle all customer service as well. With every item you sell you will be charged fees, but it is well worth it for what Amazon will do for you. Since Amazon is doing a lot of the work for you, it makes it that much easier to sell products without a lot of hastle.

Amazon FBA is a great platform to sell many different products and items in order to earn income. Books have been and continue to be one of the best things to sell. Although books do come in different sizes, most are similarly sized and shaped and easy to pack and ship through Amazon FBA. Books are very plentiful and easy to find. Most people have dozens of them lying around their homes and once they are not needed they are usually donated to thrift stores or undervalued by those owning them. There are many books that are not worth selling on Amazon FBA, quite a few are and can fetch $10, $20, $30 dollars or more consistently. I've even sold quite a few books in the $100-$150 range. The key is learning to spot which ones have potential profit. Also, since used books are so plentiful you usually can pick them up at most places for $2 or less. Some sources such as thrift stores have been raising their prices on books lately which makes it a bit more challenging to get books cheaply . But don't worry about that too much because sourcing cheap books can still be easily done. Books have a very high return on your investment (ROI). So for those that are just starting out and use the methods in this book, it will be hard to "lose" money if you do a decent job sourcing good books. Even if you make some bad purchases, since you should be buying the books so cheaply you aren't risking too much. With the tips taught in this book, you will be able to see that finding books, shipping them, and having them sell through Amazon.com is a repeatable process that can once you get the hang of can provide a consistent stream of sales and profit. As you source books and ship them in consistently Amazon this system will provide an income stream that will sometimes seem like passive income. Once you send your books to Amazon, they will pack and ship and deal with the order and customer service for you. Your job (for the most part will) be to keep looking for profitable books and sending them in!

CHAPTER 2. SCANNING BOOKS

When trying to find books to purchase for resale, you will have to be selective and find the ones that have good value and can make a profit from. Often when you find a source, such as a library sale or a thrift store, there will be hundreds of books in front of you and you may have a hard time knowing which books to purchase. This is where you will need to scan book barcodes in order to find the value and profitability of a book. The good news that you can purchase or get for free the scanning app you need on your phone to do your scanning.

A free app is the Amazon app. It will tell you basic information and it can be a good way to start out if you don't want to pay for a premium scouting app. But It is also usable for experienced sellers because it does often give the important basic info that is needed when you are deciding to purchase a book to resell on Amazon.

There are other apps that are available for a monthly fee and connect straight to Amazon's pricing info via your smartphone. FBA scan (live data) app it is available for about $10 per month and gives info on current Amazon prices, as well as sales rank info. It also has many other features as well that can be a good help. Another good app is the Profit Bandit app. These two apps give a good bang for your buck and are low priced.

When using a scanning app on your phone that is connected to the internet there are some times when your internet will be slow, or you will have trouble connecting which will slow you down. I currently am using the FBA scan app but have something called local data. I am able to connect and download all of Amazon's pricing data to my phone at home, then when I go out scanning I don't have to connect to the internet at all to scan. I find that I am able to scan books a lot faster and it is a lot more profitable this way. It does cost about $30 per month (compared to the $10 for live data), but it works out for me because I can make the money up in a couple of minutes due to its ability to allow me to scan faster.

One more thing that can really help with efficiency and speed is buying a small Bluetooth barcode scanner. These are usually about two by one inch in length and connect to your phone via Bluetooth. I actually Velcro it to the back of my phone. Instead of using the camera on your phone to scan the book, I use the barcode scanner. When I use this I am able to scan about 3x faster than if I was scanning the barcode using the camera on my phone. This set up will help you scan large volumes of books which can help increase profits. They cost about $200-$300 on average and are good to have. They are not absolutely necessary though if you don't feel you are ready to spend that type of money.

Some books will not have a barcode. If they don't you can type in the ISBN number manually which will allow the item to pop up on your scanning app as well. Once in awhile a book won't have an ISBN number or barcode. In this case you can type in the book title. Just make sure that the book you have in your hand matches what you are looking up in the Amazon system.

CHAPTER 3. BOOK SOURCING

In order to have books to sell, you must begin to find good places to source your books from. It is important to find sources where you can get books at a low price. $0-$2 for the most part, then sell it at a high enough price to make a good profit. You can buy books for more than that but remember if you are going to spend $5 to secure a book to sell, you should make sure you can sell it for a higher margin and it has a good sales ranking. Here are some of the most common sources to get books.

Thrift Type Stores-Most of the books I have sourced have com from stores such as Goodwill, Savers, Salvation Arny and other thrift stores. Although many stores such as Goodwill now sell their higher quality books online as well, there are still many profitable books available in these stores to be found. The good part with these types of places is you can source at your own convenience. I will usually go right after my regular 9-5 job or on weekends. Also in these thrift type stores, there are often half price sales and books that can be secured in the $1-2 range or less. There is always new inventory coming in as well, so it is good to make it a habit of visiting each store every so often. Each store's selection will vary. Where I live there are quite a few Goodwills, but each one is quite different and some have better pricing or selection than others. Find the best spots and frequent them the most often. Most of the books I have purchased for resale have been from stores such as Goodwill, thrift stores, and Salvation Army.

Library Book Sales-Library book sales are probably the most profitable and fastest way to secure a good amount of book inventory quickly. They are held by different libraries or groups of libraries either annually, twice a year, or quarterly. Most sales I have seen are on weekends, but some larger ones can be held even up to a full week during summer periods. Most books are usually reasonably priced $1-2 dollars and the sales will usually be organized by book categories such as Politics, Sports, History, Philosophy, Religion etc. One tip for sellers is at the end of the sale, usually the last day, books will be marked down and prices slashed either 50% off, all books 50 cents, or $5 a bag. Each bag of books you fill will be only $5. The end of a book sale is an excellent opportunity to pick up inventory at a very low price point.

Some Tips For Attending Booksales-Widely advertised (like on booksalesfound.com) and large book sales can be great. Sometimes it is good to find library book sales that are not advertised widely online or on other avenues. Many of the larger book sales that are heavily advertised have way too many booksellers already attending which makes it a bit stressful and hard to secure good books at widely advertised sales.

One good tip is to call each library in your area every so often (i.e. every 2-3 months to ask if they have any sales coming up soon). Then mark these on your calendar. Many of the smaller library sales have less advertising, so they don't have as many other people trying to find books to resell.

Be ready to buy in bulk. At a thrift store, you may be able to buy a dozen or so books and be satisfied. But it is a bit different if you are attending a library sale. There are so many books available, Taking home 100+ books or more should be common. Remember Library sales only come around every so often so be ready to buy big and in bulk.

Book sales are a bit more stressful. Everybody will be excited, especially other booksellers, to shop around. Have a plan on how you are going to secure your books, ie. A cart or dolly. Be ready for quite a few trips back and forth to your car to load your books and get some more!

Make sure you have your scanner/phone ready fully charged, as well as a backup battery recharger. If you run out of battery power you won't be able to scan and that will mess up your book sourcing day.

Show up early to the sale. You don't need to rush to be the first through the door, but don't be too late either. Make sure you are there within the first 5-10 minutes. If you come later than that you will be at a disadvantage with many other people already getting settled in and getting in on the best deals.

Attend the preview sales. This is an opportunity to secure high quality books at the sale. Some library sales will have a preview sale. It often will cost a small amount usually $25 or less to be invited to the preview sale. If the sale has a good enough selection of books it is often important to attend these. If another seller/sellers attend these, they are pretty much getting an opportunity to buy just about every high priced book available at the sale before you do. By the time the preview sale is over many of the quality will be gone.

Here are a few other great places to source books:

Ongoing friends of the library book sales/stores-There are probably dozens of public libraries in and around most communities. Many Libraries have a section where there is an ongoing library sale. During normal library hours books can be purchased with all proceeds going to the friends of the library. Often there is a small selection of books, often some will be profitable. These books have usually been donated by people who live in the community. I have quite a few of these that I go to every so often in which I am sure I have made many $1,000's in profit from over the years. A good idea would be to see which libraries have the best ongoing sales in frequent them the most often.

Estate Sales-I haven't been to many estate sales but have heard stories from some who have. I 've heard about quite a few people that have come across collections of books that are being let go in large lots at good prices. A best case scenario would be to come across a large collection/selection of profitable books and end up buying them all in bulk at a cheap price. A good idea is to get a rough idea of how much profit you could make on the lot of books and then give a good low offer that will be accepted.

Used Bookstores- Many book resellers overlook used bookstores as a good place to source books. The reason for this is probably because many figure that these bookstores already have priced their books perfectly. Since used bookstores are in the business of selling books many think there is no way you could source these places to make profit. There are a few reasons why this can be totally wrong. One reason is that not all of these bookstores price competitively at Amazon prices. If they are selling a book for $5 in their store and it sells for $30 on Amazon, it's possible you could scoop that book up and make a profit. Another thing is that sometimes great books slip through the cracks at these stores and for some reason at least 5% of the books in the store could be bought and flipped for profit. I believe that to be able to selling books from used bookstores can be a bit more challenging from because there is a narrower window for you to pick up gems. As with anything though, just give it a try find some strategies and see if you can extract some good books from this source. You may be surprised with the profits what you can walk away with.

Garage/Rummage Sales- The good news about these is that you often can find very profitable books that the owners are selling at very low prices. Often the owners have undervalued the book and are just trying to get rid of it. Some of these garage type sales (especially moving sales) have people practically giving away of entire collections of books in which you can come in and buy it at pennies on the dollar. The bad news is that sometimes you can go to a sale and there are no good books (or any books) for sale. So the chance of your wasting time is a bit higher.

Ebay- This is an interesting source. Ebay can work but keep in mind many other people are looking for deals on Ebay as well. My experience with Ebay hasn't been as profitable as many of the other sources listed in this book. If you are not able to find many sources of books in your area, you may want to give Ebay a try. What you will want to do is buy books low on the Ebay platform and sell it high on Amazon.

Private Sellers and Craigslist Ads-Give these a try as well, use every possible angle you can to secure your books!

There are dozens of other ways to find books to sell, but these are some that are the most common. I really believe that at the end it isn't always where you get your books that is most important (although it is somewhat). What's most important is that you find good books where ever you can. Not all sources will last forever. Your favorite used bookstore may go out of business. You need to have a good plethora of sources that will keep the income flowing continually, so always be researching and keeping a good look out for them.

There are quite a few people that have gone on book sourcing road trips and vacations. This is when you drive or even fly to other towns/states and begin sourcing on the road. You would spend some time on vacation, and pay for much of the trip expenses taking some of the time to source books. If you have a laptop as well as a printer, you can connect to hotel Wi-Fi and do it all in your hotel room. For this to work you have to have a good plan on where you are going to source because often you are going into unknown territory.

An important thing I do is keep a source log. In a source log I might have a list of all the sources I can find books at and their location. It's important to be systematic with this. You can find some good books to sell now and then and make a few bucks. If you really want to make good income make sure that you have a source log and systemize your sourcing routine. Some sources you might visit weekly. Some monthly and some annually or quarterly. Unless you have a good system and are consistent You will be leaving money on the table guaranteed.

Lastly there will be competition when sourcing books. That would be, other people that have the same idea of reselling books just like you. Even though there are people out there that know what they are doing, you would be surprised on how many who don't. In my own experience I have seen many people come and go who no longer resell books for some reason. I often see people that are finding books at places like thrift stores who are selling on places like Ebay instead. So even though you will have competition don't worry. Just do the best that you can and there are plenty of books out there to source.

CHAPTER 4. BEST TYPES OF BOOKS TO RESELL

There are millions of different books out there to purchase. From my experience at least 90% of them that you find will not bring any profit selling on Amazon FBA. It's just a fact that as a book reseller you will be looking for hidden gems and treasures within the mass piles of books you will see at thrift stores, library sales etc. The way you will find these profitable books is you will scan them to see their sales price on Amazon as well as see the sales rank of how well it usually sells. The other way is that over time and the more you scout for books the better you will be at picking up with your eyes which books might have good value and which ones to stay away from.

The books I focus on are almost all nonfiction. I rarely look for fiction. From what I have experienced, for every 20 books that are nonfiction and are good sellers on Amazon FBA only about 1 or less of a fiction book would have good profit value. This is because MSRP on nonfiction books often are $25, $39.95, $49.95 etc. MSRP on textbooks often are $100 or more usually as well. This means that if an original price on a textbook is $149. I could easily sell it used for $35 or so and the buyer would be happy. I would have probably picked the book up for $2-3 so my profit would be great. Most fiction books sell new for about $16.99 or less and the value tends to drop under $10 quickly. So unless it is a fairly new fiction book, it will probably not bring back enough profit to be worth sourcing.

One of the key things to remember is that selling textbooks on FBA is one of the most lucrative things that can be done. You can't just sell "any textbook" for a good profit, but there are many out there that can give great returns. College students have to pay enormous amounts of money each year on very expensive textbooks for their college classes. They often will buy them new or used from their college bookstore which can be very pricey. This is where you can come in and capitalize on their need. Sometimes students choose for whatever reason to purchase the textbooks they need on Amazon.com. The amazing thing I have found is that during the time students are going back to college before a semester starts (starting around January and also around August) students will buy textbooks in droves.This is called textbook season and If you have a ton of textbooks you have purchased at a cheap price, they will sell for great, and often during this time of year. I have found that many, many textbooks even up to 10 years old will sell for good prices during this time as well as throughout the year. I will sell many textbooks for upwards of $25 consistently and up to around $125 used and see them sell very well.

Any academic type book can also be a good seller. Especially books by any college press such as Princeton University Press, Stanford University Press etc. Some of these colleges print books on obscure academic topics that become very "in demand" during January and August textbook season. Students and academic people need these books for college and will usually pay $15 or more for these sort of books. These sort of books sometimes don't have the best sales rank, but books like these tend to hold their value well and can be good investments when sourced for $2 or less.

Just keep in mind that most books (more than 90%) will not make you any profit on Amazon FBA, a major key principle is not to waste too much time on what is known not to sell. Anything that is produced for the masses and woefully outdated is usually a no-no and usually not something that is sellable for profit. If you are new to finding books to source it may take some time to get the hang of what types of books you are looking to buy, but once you begin to see patterns over time you will get a better understanding of what you are looking for. It is actually a good thing that 90% of books aren't profitable for the most part. If it was super easy to sell books online everyone without a good strategy would be doing this. With the tips in this book hopefully you will become one of the few that can find profitable books.

CHAPTER 5. BOOK SALES RANK AND PRICING ON AMAZON

Every time a book on Amazon sells, Amazon tracks the sale. Each time you search for a book on your scanning app you will see that it has a rank. Books that you find could have a rank of 1 all the way up to over 10 million. If a book has "no rank" on your app that means it has never sold a copy on Amazon before. Meaning most of the time it is not a book you would usually want to sell.

Let's just say there is a book on "Filipino Recipes" and it might be ranked 1.5 million today. A 1.5 million rank in books isn't horribly bad , but it isn't that great either. It might sell tomorrow and the rank could drop to around 150,000. If the book does not sell for quite a while the rank would continue to go higher and higher until it sells again. A book that is ranked very low might sell hundreds of copies on Amazon EACH DAY. Some books with high Amazon rank might only sell one copy a month, or even year. Sales rank is great and can really help you get some clues on how fast a book "might" sell.

Amazon sales rank though isn't a 100% perfect gauge of a book's demand because if say, a book was ranked 3.5 million (hardly ever sells). If that books sells TODAY, the rank might drop to 400,000 (a good rank). This data might trick you into thinking the book is a very good seller, but it isn't. It just has a good rank RIGHT NOW because it just sold a copy. This is okay though because even though this can happen with sales rank from time to time, the data sales rank gives is usually on point, and is very important and useful.

When looking for a book to resell two important things you REALLY want to know is if you can sell the book for a good profit (buy low and sell high) and if the book has a good sales rank (it will sell). The best of both worlds would be that you find a book that sells for a high price AND has a good sales rank. I have my own strategy that you may want to consider. I will buy a book that sells for $9 or more on FBA if it has a sales rank of under 1 million. I usually do not purchase books that sell on FBA for less than $9 because at this point would rather focus on books that will bring more of a profit. I will sometimes sell books that cost between $8-9 but am doing it less because the profit margin is a bit slim. It is up to you if you would like to sell books on FBA for less than I do, but I would not advise you to list books for less than $8 on FBA because after you pay for the book (sourcing cost), pay for shipping it to Amazon, and pay Amazon fees, there won't be enough profit margin to make it worth your while.

I believe that 1 million is the end point of a GOOD sales rank. From my experience books under one million have the potential to sell in not too long a time. I will often buy books ranked 1 million to 2 million as well. With these sort of books, I try to make sure that I potentially can sell these For at least $12-14 or more on FBA because some of these may not sell for a while and if I am going to be waiting a bit longer for these types of books to sell I would like to get more money back from them. I will buy books ranked 2 million to 3 million as well. Sales rank between 2 and three million I will buy as well if I am seeing that the book will sell for around $20 or more. Any book ranked more than 3 million is a risk in my book. I would not buy MANY books ranked 3 million or more. I will buy a few of these once in a while if it is worth about $30 or more and I can pick it up for around $2 or less. The reasoning behind this is that if I buy 10 books ranked 3 million or more for $1 each (a $10 investment), and actually just sell one of them for say $45. I will have doubled my investment already and whatever else of these end up selling is pure profit. You may end up
having a strategy that might be a little bit different than mine it all depends on what you are comfortable with.

One thing you need to consistently do is price your books competitively. A smart thing to do is try to come with a good
idea of what is the most you think a person would pay for your book. You are selling your book through the FBA program and you will be pricing your book to compete against other FBA sellers. Remember that if you price your books lower you WILL sell them faster but you will probably, make less money because it is likely you will be getting less profit. Often times you may want to see what others are selling the same book for through merchant fulfilled (on your scanning app) but remember that you can price your books much higher through FBA than if you were selling the book through merchant fulfilled.

Another thing that is really important is repricing your books. Prices fluctuate on each book all the time and when sales are made. You want to make sure your books are priced competitively enough. You want to make sure you don't price too low, but also that you don't price too high. Over the past two years, I have begun to understand the value of books much better and have become very good at pricing my books. When I first started out though I had some trouble. Many people price their books to be the lowest price, which can help you get more sales which is great. I believe it's good at times to be the lowest price, but if I believe I can get a few dollars more in the long run pricing my book a bit higher I will do this as well. Some sellers use a repricer. This is a software that will change your price on our books automatically to keep your prices competitive. I for myself do not use a repricer but many people do. It may be something you want to consider, but do some research on it first.

When you end up sending your books in to Amazon many people will be surprised when they find out that not all of their books will sell within the first few days or even months. The reason for this is that there are millions of books out there and people don't purchase (as a general rule) books as often as they purchase everyday necessities such toothpaste, gas, groceries, etc. Patience is a key as well as "trusting the process". I would focus on sending in quality books as well as getting a good amount of inventory into the FBA warehouses. If some of your books don't sell after a year or so, I would suggest that sometimes, lowering your price is the right thing to do. But here is an important tip. Many of the books that can be the most profitable will take the longest to sell. Let's just say you found a book that is worth $175 on Amazon for $1 at the thrift store. Not many people will pay $175 for a book. You may need to wait a year for the right person to buy it at that price. This may be a long wait but when it sells the wait will be totally worth it. At a certain point you will probably have at least over 500 books in your inventory. I've heard of people that have had over 50,000 books in their inventory (they are full time sellers of course).

CHAPTER 6. BOOK GRADING AND CONDITION

When buying books it is important to know how to grade your books and understand the condition they are in. When you list your books to sell on Amazon FBA you must rate your books based on the actual condition. A book can be rated as New, Very Good, Good, or Acceptable. It is very important to grade your book accurately for everyone's sake. If a buyer believes that you sent them a book that is improperly graded they can give you negatively feedback that will affect your seller rating, which is NOT GOOD.

I will go over my understanding of what I have learned myself as a bookseller as well as what I have learned from others, on how to grade a book.

NEW CONDITION- This is a book that is in mint condition. Books will sometimes have the shrink wrap on them so these are obviously new. Most of the time though you will not be sure if a book has not been read. I usually will not grade a book new unless it is flawless.

VERY GOOD CONDITION-This is a book that has a little bit of wear. The cover is still usually glossy with no bends or major wear to the book. Also I will look inside and make sure that there
is no highlighting or writing. This is a book that is close to new but obviously not new.

GOOD CONDITION-This is the condition that I grade most of the books, because this is the average condition of most books. Good condition books can have more of a dull cover (gloss is gone) some writing or highlighting within. I check that it's on less than 5% of the pages just to be on the safe side. The book will have obvious wear although nothing major that stands out.

ACCEPTABLE CONDITION-This is a book with major wear and some highlighting. It is important though to note that if the book has very heavy wear or falling apart, you should not sell it. If pages are ripped or missing you should not sell it as well. The smart thing to do is think, "would I be happy receiving a book this worn out?" Sometimes a book will be selling at a very high price and you may be tempted to sell it even though it's in very horrible condition. Don't be tempted, it isn't worth it. If the book has too much writing highlighting I would bypass it as well. I sell about 20% of my books in acceptable condition and they can be profitable.

When you source books they will sometimes have price stickers on them. Make sure you remove these before sending them in. Also remember that you are actually taking books in from different sources and reselling them as "your books" on your Amazon seller account. I often will check if the books I buy need to have the covers cleaned and wiped off a bit (I will use handi wipes) to make them more presentable when they are received by my Amazon customers.

Every seller on Amazon has a seller feedback rating. The highest rating that can be achieved is 100% feedback rating. You want to make sure that you stay at or near 100%. If you are a buyer would you most likely buy from a seller with 99% rating or 78%? The higher rating of course! Every person that buys a book from you on Amazon has an opportunity to give you a rating from 1-5 based on their transaction, a 5 or 4 rating is positive. 3 is neutral. 2 to 1 is considered negative. Since Amazon is handling most of the customer service you don't have a lot to be concerned about regarding dealing with customers. What you need to make sure of is that you grade your books correctly and send the right books in. Make sure the book you are sending in to Amazon is the book the customer expects. If you are advertising your book as Biology 10th Edition. Make
Sure that you don't send in Biology 9th Edition. Even if you made an honest mistake sending in the wrong book, you still can be hit with a negative feedback.

Sometimes a buyer will give you a feedback that is unfair. The good news is that Amazon is pretty good at removing negative feedback if it is unfair and inappropriate. For example a buyer might give a negative because the book was "not a good read and pretty boring". This can be removed by Amazon because it is a book review and has nothing to do with customer experience. If you want to apply to have a negative feedback removed you can ask Amazon in the remove feedback page on your Amazon seller account.

CHAPTER 7. PACKING AND SHIPPING YOUR BOOKS

After you have secured some books you are ready to sell (at least 25). You will want to create a shipment and send them into Amazon. You will need some packing tape, a sturdy shipping box that will fit your books, as well as some AVERY or similar type labels, and printer hooked up to your computer. You will need to go into your seller account on Amazon.com and "add product" to your inventory. You will then list each book one by one into your inventory. Then within the manage inventory tab, you will mark all the books you are sending in your shipment Then click on send/replenish inventory. Each book you send in will need to have a sticker on the back. These stickers will be available as you are creating your shipment .This sticker is an avery sized label that goes on the back of each book. You can either put a label on each book yourself or Amazon will give you the option where they will do it for a small fee. After you have logged in your shipment, Amazon will have an address label for you to print out, where they would like you to send the shipment. So the main things you need are shipping boxes, tape, labels, as well as your printer. I would advise you to start off simply and as you get more familiar with listing and creating shipments, begin to scale up and get better equipment such as a Dymo label printer, barcode scanner, listing software, etc. When I first started out I tried to be as cheap as possible in buying and getting my supplies. Do you know what I think now? Well, I still think your best bet is to stay cheap if you are a part time seller. Get your boxes for free or at home depot. Get economy type tape as well. If you are going into full time selling I would change up a bit and sure you run your bookselling as a more serious operation and be more professional (buy supplies in bulk, upgrade your supplies etc.).

I'm just going to be real with you. Listing, packing and shipping books into Amazon for me is probably the least fun part about book selling. If you are like me you will have all the books you sourced in random piles in your house. You then need to process them and get them shipped into Amazon. There is nothing glorious about this process, but it must be done consistently if you are going to make money. If you buy 100 awesome books dirt cheap with great profit potential, how much will you make if they are sitting in your house? You won't make a dime! So they have got to be shipped in to Amazon as quick as you can in order to get back your investment as well as produce profit.

CHAPTER 8. CONCLUSION

This book was written to be a short introduction and outline on how to sell books on Amazon FBA. Hopefully, you have learned some of the basics of what it takes to make a good side income selling books (or full time if you so wish!). Also for those who are seasoned book sellers on Amazon or have some experience, hopefully you learned a few nuggets here and there that will help you increase your business as well. I have found that once you actually start to implement the process and send your first few book shipments into Amazon and see some sales, you will get more and more understanding of what works and how to make this very profitable. Although I have been selling books for quite a while I believe there are always things to learn and ways to improve my bookselling business. There are many things over time I heard other booksellers doing that I just but ignored their advice because, my way was working just fine! But as I implemented some of what others were doing and suggesting I increased my income.

Here is a major tip for you, even if you have been selling a long time. Go to youtube.com and type in FBA bookselling, or Amazon bookselling or anything similar. As the first page or two of videos pop up start to learn from those that are giving tips and tricks about many of the things I taught in this book. When I first started I was a bit intimidated by all the rules and procedures Amazon has that you need to follow to sell products with them online. I didn't get down every procedure all at once but got better and understood more as I read articles and watch tutorial videos on Amazon and on youtube. In this short book, I am not able to teach you every nook and cranny of what to do, but one thing I learned is you almost might be able to learn almost anything watching youtube videos! There are quite a few people that have youtube channels that pop up that are full time booksellers that are giving much of the advice you need. If they have over 1,000 youtube subscribers and they are talking about books in most of their videos it might be a good idea to study what they are saying and think about implementing it. There are also some other FBA youtube gurus that also good advice about selling books although some don't focus mainly on bookselling. Also if you need thanks information on a certain topic you could type in "FBA book repricing" or "FBA book sourcing" etc, to learn more. But again remember that you must slowly implement what you learn and actually execute it to continue to gain more understanding and true depth of knowledge. One of the things I like to do while I'm busy packing book shipments is turn on youtube and listen to a few videos as I'm working.

So I hope you enjoyed the book and remember to keep learning, executing, and growing in your bookselling!

BONUS!

Here is a secret master list of Sources where you may be able to find used books

1. Thrift stores
2. Rummage sales
3. Library Booksales
4. Craigslist
5. Estate sales
6. Law offices (often have law books that they no longer need
7. College students
8. Contact thrift stores if you can buy/get there books wholesale or take some of their extra books
9. Clearance racks at major bookstore retailers
10. Advertise online, or in your area that you are buying books

11. Booksales found(search for upcoming book sales
12. Call all local libraries and find where they will be having booksales
13. In store library book sales (during library hours)
14. Family and friends
15. Often other amazon booksellers are giving up selling on Amazon. Find who they are and buy their inventory
16. Post your own ads on craigslists that you are buying books
17. Ebay
18. Online surplus auctions
19. Used bookstores
20. Get in contact with local universities either libraries or somewhere on campus there may be books that no longer are needed
21. High schools and Elementary schools purge books constantly to update their curriculum
22. Recycling center
23. Flea markets/swap meets
24. Estate sales
25. Dumpster diving (many libraries/thrift stores) throw away books that still have profit
26. Storage Auctions
27. Surplus/Closeout stores
28. Church Sales
29. Teachers/Professors
30. Anyone who is studying for a certain career and has books and textbooks they no longer need
31. Home schooling parents (have homeschooling curriculum they no longer need
32. Make business cards letting others know you buy books
33. Advertise you buy books on bulletin boards
34. Advertise on Social media
35. Foreclosures
36. Advertiser in classified ads
37. College campus bookstores
38. Open a location where others can sell you books
39. Any store that is going out of business may have books
40. Auctions

41. Trash (I once found a bunch of great books in a pile someone was throwing away (no need to get dirty..unless you want to)
42. Remainder distributors
43. USPS auctions
44. Any store that sells used items
45. Your own books you have at home

ONE LAST THING!

If you believed you recieved some value from this book I would kindly ask that you consider leaving a book review right after you read this (there should be an option to review right after reading this page). Thanks again for taking the time to read my book!

Made in the USA
Monee, IL
31 December 2021